Museum Made of Breath

Poems by Lori Brack

Kansas City   Spartan Press   Missouri

Spartan Press
Kansas City, Missouri
spartanpresskc.com

Copyright (c) Lori Brack, 2018
First Edition 1 3 5 7 9 10 8 6 4 2
ISBN: 978-1-946642-51-6
LCCN: 2018943070

Design, edits and layout: Jason Ryberg
Cover and title page images: Mri-Pilar
Author photo: Maggie Mae
All rights reserved. No part of this publication may be reproduced or transmitted in any form or by any means, electronic or mechanical, including photocopying, recording or by info retrieval system, without prior written permission from the author.

Spartan Press would like to thank Prospero's Books, The Fellowship of N-finite Jest, The Prospero Institute of Disquieted P/o/e/t/i/c/s, Will Leathem, Tom Wayne, Jeanette Powers, j. d. tulloch, Jon Bidwell, Jason Preu, Mark McClane, Tony Hayden and the whole Osage Arts Community.

Many thanks to the publications where these poems appeared, sometimes in slightly different forms:

"At the Museum of Keys," "The Luminosity of Objects," "Ylem and Plenum and Saxifrage" – *Gingko Tree Review*
"Instructions for What Comes Next" – *Miracle Monocle*
"At the Museum of Rain," "At the Museum of Trees"
– *Another Chicago Magazine*
"Delicious" – *concis*
"An Overture," "Art History"– *Moon City Review*
"Dearest Little L," "Letter to Virginia"
                – *Sugared Water: Epistolary*
"At the Museum of Flowers," "Not Yet Flying"
                – *Begin Again: 150 Kansas Poems*
"At the Museum of Possibility," "Ologies," "Some of the Rooms in the Hall of Desire" – *The Prose Poem Project*
"Vo Ed" – *North American Review*

And deep gratitude: to Heather, Mary Jane, Ric, Robin and Christopher, mi querida Maria, to Ernesto, Pilar, Harley, Patricia, Pam, to Linda, Frank and Mary, Chris, Berta and Gregg, Saralyn, Ann, Shelley, Katrina, Judy, Nancy, Jennifer, Mary, NancyJo, James, Suzanne and Bruce. To you, and to all of you unnamed who held me, here.

CONTENTS

Ylem and Plenum and Saxifrage / 1

Turning It Over / 2

Instructions for What Comes Next / 4

Novel Reading / 5

Dresses for Dancing / 6

Louise Fixes Lunch / 7

The curator of flower demise / 8

Plum Elegy / 9

Carnivore / 11

Does Not Eat, But Hungers / 12

At the Museum of Rain / 13

At the Snow Museum / 14

A Natural History of Leaves and Rivers / 15

as confirmation – echo – / 21

Joseph Cornell Takes a Bath / 22

Frida Kahlo Eats a Bean / 23

She Named His Coming / 24

Delicious / 26

Instead of Air / 27

An Overture / 28

If a Letter Was Part of Air / 29

Kansas Girl / 30

Field / 31

How in winter the haunting is done / 32

Farm Wife / 33

If they don't tell us / 34

Art History / 35

Dearest Little L, / 36

At the Museum of Flowers / 37

World to Come / 38

In the Book of Old Pictures / 39

Not Yet Flying / 40

In the Book of Marvels / 42

At the Museum of Possibility / 43

Ologies / 44

There are no minor gods / 45

The Luminosity of Objects / 46

Some of the Rooms in the Hall of Desire / 47

Letter to Virginia / 48

The Mortal Takes Herself Home / 49

Vo Ed / 50

At the Museum of Keys / 51

At the Museum of Trees / 52

At the Museum of Lost Things / 53

If only once the summons were a roar / 54

Each November Day / 55

The museum man!
I wish he'd take Pa's spitbox!
I'm going to take that spitbox out
and bury it in the ground
and put a stone on top.
Because without that stone on top
it would come back.

-Lorine Niedecker

Ylem and Plenum and Saxifrage

Before I could read, I consumed. Upside down under
the willow I turned the words in my father's books and
pronounced each meaning before I knew a single letter.

My mother vacuumed the blue and green carpet every day.
She insisted the world must be emptied — as if she could
— of its ashes, its gravel from the path, its leafy remains.

Genus of whiplash, yellow mountain, tumbling waters. You
send your clingy toes down. You believe this earth, its cobwebs,
delicate rosettes, heavily silvered, hidden by the velvety fur.

Turning It Over

By letter, a psychic offers
to help me discover whether
I am under a spell. This
is why I bury my fingernail
parings, the hair from my brush:
to avoid curses and the higgledy-
piggledy distribution of my dna.
Seems that might not have been
enough. The psychic says
my spell is blue,
comes from afar, smells
like old butter. Besides
reciting to her the number
on my mastercard, I should
drink a tea made of dandelion
at midnight for the next seven
days, put my left foot first
on the floor when I awake,
eat nothing but yellow fruit
each Sunday until the next
full moon, stop singing in the car
(how did she know?) and drop
twenty one-dollar coins under trees
in anonymous front lawns all over
town every Wednesday

for a solid month. I will know
the spell is broken when
I look into the mirror and find
the mark of June upon my
cheek: a pink, kiss-shaped
stain that signifies the blessing
of summer and banishment of sadness,
weight gain, underemployment.
It is day two.

Instructions for What Comes Next

First, give up all you thought you knew. Then open your breathless chest. Look in. Find the single thing you came here with, attached by only a string. If it is shopworn, treat it tenderly. If it sparkles, put your fingerprints all over it. Call it by its secret name. Give it a drink of water in the night. When lightning flashes through the window, you will discover its arm outside the covers, cradling you in its grasp.

Novel Reading

5 a.m.

Except for the weathercock sunrise (more literature than somnambulist in the hedge), I want to be the only reader inspecting the verges. Here, maybe, are little blackcurrants of tantrum. I am the eyewitness, snuffling up each black synonym, each pigtail of punctuation. The filament itself begins to move, not anticlimax as I expected, but fabrication, a seedbed of sequin as if the world had red in it.

11 p.m.

I want to be alone when I discover the wildcat rosebud, the thingamabob itself, to feel the bivouac of stubborn grammar. Liaisons enter and I pick out the partings with my fingerprint, malleable flex. My thistle petticoats gather condolence. Sandstorms ravage the sheer. One wound falls away and I reel toward the garnet, piggyback, brushing the sanitarium out of my skirt. *Someone* had to do it.

Dresses for Dancing

1
Needle plummeting, its dance holding breath,
she stitches her first camouflage against trouble.
Tough minuet of catch and bind, strokes
map umbilical connections taut and fine,
embroidery her mother trained her to.

2
She walks into night through the back door,
dark hanging near as the brink of fall.
She unbuttons the costumes of who
she has been, pulls her arms from each
swallowing sleeve, swears these dresses defy mending.

3
White lace music and dress plunging back,
her underwings cushion a dream of dancing.
He asks her to invent a way to fly, but they
stumble mid-step, let go, forget — her arms
sprouting feathers for plummeting.

Louise Fixes Lunch

To be an artist is a guarantee to your fellow humans that the wear and tear of living will not let you become a murderer.

– Louise Bourgeois, sculptor

Surely my mother bred me
to cut strawberries, to watch them
unfold in a white bowl, pieces
falling open, four chambers of the red
heart. Sometimes I put them onto the table
whole and bite off the flesh, discard
the leaves. I come into the studio
like a strawberry, my heart
waiting for the knife. Instead, I pound
and saw at the white stone. A strawberry

is symbolic by being only itself, fat
and red, sized to a woman's palm, begging
to be broken into. Maybe an insect
would sip at the ragged edge.
My heart does not give up
its red though I stab and twist, halve
it and halve again. These hands
were bred by my father to serve
him. Instead I have set out my heart.

The curator of flower demise

lights little wax votives for petals,
sepals, secret deep tongues
where lily's manufacture seeps.
She keeps bottles and jars
with screw tops and stoppers,
glass sequesters of tomato blossom
equally white and deep green,
lilac's heavy lavender, something red
that reminds her of the French aunts.
Jasmine says one paper label.
Vervain replies another. A going
toward the wet garden, a gate.

Plum Elegy

Gnats die in the creases of my arms,
around my waist. My braid sticks
in brush. I yank it free
till it is loose, torn as my hands

reaching across thorns for this fruit.
My car leans into the ditch.
I ignore its air-conditioned invitation
calling me above plums' thud

in the bucket, whine of flies and heat's
hiss in my ears. I learned this place
from my mother's summer rounds and
watch it carefully. Some years, drought

makes plums hard and sparse. Some years,
jays and starlings get here first when I have not
cared sweet enough to stake my claim
or risk hanging pie tins in someone else's brush.

Near here's the missing house
where she grew up, gone
to a clump of iris, concrete cellar walls.
Cows graze where she slept.

She left this lost house to marry, to move
to town, to wait fourteen years
for me. I have her picture. Velvet
violets on green fabric stems are pinned

at the neck of her white blouse
billowed with my beginning,
her lipstick the brightest thing
in the room. But I never learned.

I stopped at picking
and ignored the pitting, boiling,
skimming, sweetening, pouring
it takes to make this sharp fruit food.

Like the practice of relation
I reach again among the thorns.
I twist, pull them free, take
this fruit between my fingers, hoard

plums here in boxes in the car, drive
with the live red smell of them
faster down the sandy road
than my mother's fancy could bear.

Carnivore

I have never been a fox run down
in a field though I remember
the fleeing panic. Boys one summer
mistook me for a girl and landed hard
grapes against my neck. I darted
and a decade on I ran from a lurker,
crashing backyards in the dark.
I dashed, too, from a hawk
swooping out of cedars — small
lesson in being prey. Oh, I know
there is a bloody row behind me.
I drag with every step a gory parade
of bodies I have consumed. Bloody
would be a blessing next to unstrung
intestines spilling shit after the killing
hammer. With every bite I am
brutal, made and sustained. And if
that is so, then what is a robin
with its beak full of worm? Mine
does not wriggle. Or flee. I've been
reading the world all wrong — the *an*
at the end of human is the *an*
at the beginning of animal, the one
I want to be: sloth lazy, up on my hind
paws, waiting for someone to bring
whoever we're having for dinner.

Does Not Eat, But Hungers

Hansel, who very much liked the taste of the roof, tore down another large piece, and Gretel poked out an entire round windowpane.

– Jacob & Wilhelm Grimm

I should cry nibble, nibble, irresistible as I am. When it
rained, I felt my melting, called her bitch until she would
pat and bustle, oven-warm, and make me new. Between
visitors, I heard her in there, mother hag, rattling pans
and breathing rough all over the sugar glass. I ask you,
which would you rather eat: my confectionary or the fatty
roasting scream and moan? I'm sure she's dead this time,
beaten by a little girl and a chicken's bone. I knew that hen.
I felt her appetite pecking around my brittle footing.
In the village they call me Hexenhaus but only chickens
and children called me food. So for my delectability,
here I stand — chicken fricasseed, mother baked, plump
children flown. Why do they call me cake when no one
lives on sweet alone?

At the Museum of Rain

A work of art is a world. The museum, a world of worlds, a morsel of the infinite.

- Marc-Antoine Mathieu

All the careful labels are running ink. Downpour encroaches on light drizzle's exhibit space. Someone complains that thunder interrupts his contemplation of rolling mist. The guards must help two visitors from Sonora to the door once they discover the meaning of sprinkle and begin pouring rivulets of tears. All the umbrellas turn up missing.

At the Snow Museum

Walkers sidestep the revolving door once they catch a whiff of what's inside. Constant winter blusters behind glass, blowing flakes the size of a baby's palm or small and sharp as shards of sky. You remember. Yellow light blurs the icy kitchen window and red boots squeak as you follow her down the middle of the slippery street. It is later than you've ever been. Or earlier. In the streetlight, snow swarms like summer moths. White tracks fill up behind you.

A Natural History of Leaves and Rivers

Two landscapes make a pair of hanging veils:

We do not need
the path of light
across the water. We
are not merely feral.
We do not turn our backs,
do not follow its arrow.

> Boats of our bloodline, born for paddling,
> whose hundred suits
> of clothes do we wear?

We cast off, pull in the chain,
in our pockets only a pair
of coins and a rare stamp
from a country we forgot.

*

I walked the river's current

> Ancient word for stone, for hand,
> for some of the ways
> the river under the visible
> river guides me.

Together we plan an experiment.
Our apparatus: mirror
and laughter, red fruit in a milky bowl,
envelopes and not quite enough
money. We explore
the second story on stocking feet
where morning rooms glow —
toast and jam, wet shirt drying
over the chair back. I wash
my hands with soap we bought
somewhere exotic, each white lozenge
wrapped in its pink paper nest.

> *The lines begin to settle,*
> *to whisper*

> A poem is not
> unlike math, in which you
> solve for X, but almost every
> noun and verb seem an X to her.

You row while I do this;
keep your back to the task
while I continue with our sea chronicle.
I'm up to the part
where I list the invisible fish.

*

Those two, or is it four?
>	I've watched them grow
>	and grow apart. They
>	believe in miles the way
>	they once minded their mother.
>	All the pretty things started
>	there. I have the documents.
>	This one says: *You is both*
>	*singular and plural.*
>	Line them up like candies,
>	each sweet sorted by flavor,
>	and touch each one,
>	disarrange the sugar dusting,
>	lick your fingers.

>	Much knowing comes through
>	flesh, though we privilege
>	distances of sight.

In physics, observer effect means changes
that noticing makes in whatever is being seen.

>	When you read along,
>	each word finds its way
>	to your tongue, fleshy lobe
>	of language and eating.
>	Remember the spoon whittled

       at the campfire? Use it for the dull
       and shallow tool it was,
       dipper of air. You'd go hungry
       with only grammar's meager meal.

She could never
leave most things
alone.

*

Here's evidence to prove what I say is true:

       tiny kicking black
       back legs of a tadpole

       cool white cream
       slips from spoon to tongue

       your fingers holding
       the lost picture of your mother,
       her belly round with what will be you.

*

What wild
and unattended daughters,
sips of freedom and no one's son —
tent village ring, my face smoke and wind
blurred, bites from the black iron pot.

Caught, my braids unfurl rainwater,
tree conversation, sleeping bag dark.
Someone's father
guards the gate.
Lock and chain whisper as though the forest
can be kept out, ringed by river
where I walk the current
dislodging an ancient word
for stone, for hand, over
my vast and flattened land
of fires. Iron pot, pebble scrubbed.

*

      Shiny fish, transparent body
      and visible bones, a dimestore
      fishbowl, ceramic ruin,
      floating fronds of water plant.

You

      dissolved your coin
      into the bright body
      swimming there.

Mine

      I spent on licorice babies
      sorted and swallowed one-by-one,
      those sugar babes adrift
      in the boat of my blood.

My bones turn and stir.

I say: Words from my vast anthropology
And you reply: We do not need the path of light.

> *You row while I do this*

as confirmation – echo –

Long beating down the flaws with work and words, I surface
into time. That's where sun sparkles on top of ripples,
the blue of no-land-in-sight where time spreads and
glimmers. You thought time was depths, unknown
soundings where you must wear animal feet to move.
I'm not going to argue here. This is my claim: I needed
to lie back and let water hold me, to watch the sun, feel its
retinal singe, curse its way of showing everything, too lavish
with its glare. In water, you can't throw up your hands. Try it,
and find yourself sinking again, vision and breath blunted.
You're not made for diving no matter how much apparatus
you carry. You understand how easily it expires, its meter
always running out. Your only chance is time's long float
where days come unhooked and all your scars — the ones
already written and the wounds yet to come — well,
someone looks through the sky's lens and reads them all.

Joseph Cornell Takes a Bath

Before the coffin's wood embrace, Joseph sinks into the tub that stands on four lion paws. The tub opens its body to his body, all bony bruisability. He sits inside without water first, studying his toes and the shapes of his knees, watching summer fill up the second floor. Joseph's remarkable fingers turn the tap, release the stopper, turn the tap again in a rotation of filling and draining to sense the ticklish creep of water rising and falling and rising against his rippling skin.

Frida Kahlo Eats a Bean

That one. The single jewel-red and glistening bean shaped
like some esoteric spare part rolling around on her plate.
Frida's rings clink against themselves and the fork she uses
to take aim with four silver spears she calls appendix,
thirteenth rib, tailbone, Darwin's point — all our little left-
overs. The bean holds up under her assault, manages
its shape all the way to her mouth where it surrenders its
lean calories to fuel a single brushstroke: that one — her pet
monkey's miniscule ear.

She Named His Coming

> *for Jean Tatlock, who introduced the poetry*
> *of John Donne to her lover, J. Robert Oppenheimer*

She lived, too — the smart woman
out of her time, the woman
whose intelligence set her
apart for men like him, men
whose hands held her gentle,
accustomed as they were to paper.

He wrote upon her as he wrote
into the desert, as Donne
wrote — all death, all
heightened beauty — sex
and physics humming
a poetry of transcendence.

Brushing, both of them, against
something greater than their own
flesh: each other, art, visions
of fire, meddling in myth not lost
on these children of privilege
raised up under a better sky.

Passing into myth now, name
of the blast called Trinity
after her, after God, after him —
the one who mattered, whose life
granted him a quiet death
in spite of those he engineered

at Jornado del Muerto, the deaths
he is famous for. She died
drugged, bleeding in a bathtub —
whoever goes to shroud her do no harm.
Between them the sparks that flared
in poetry and The Bomb, synapses

hungry for sensation, for the world,
cold blue ink and ungodly heat —
without each they were impossible.

Delicious

The rind flat on the pavement is by chance a circle — whole but empty where she shimmied out of her skin-tight skin. Around the corner, naked Clementine hangs out on a concrete ledge. She would swing her legs if she had any, puckered around her empty center, bold as anything under the sun's blaze. When night turns cold, Clementine shivers her regret for peeling off there in the street, wishes she had not left so loose her spicy attire behind. She is sticky-sweet and irresistible to the wasp, his gold tooth shine disappearing inside.

Instead of Air

My heart tips sideways like a tilt-a-whirl,
its axis wild, swinging away from true,
and I thought gravity began with you.

They say the brain is where balance resides,
(my heart rolls sideways like a tilt-a-whirl)
but I fall crashing up against the sky

and wind tears out the meaning of my breath.
They say the brain is where balance resides,
now simple breathing feels akin to death —

just me alone up here without a net
where wind tears out the meaning of my world.
My heart veers sideways on this tilt-a-whirl.

An Overture

Your nakedness against the white sink
fragile as a box of letters in a burning room.
You bend over the bowl of water, squint
into a foggy mirror giving back
smooth shapes of shoulders, neck,
face. You could be anyone. Your hands
on the keys, fingers full of sudden
beauty — once — I listened to fire
consume old pianos, ravishing their strings.
The world unturned, heaved up its ash
for us to sift, to save what remains,
our bodies holding here — just holding.

If a Letter Was Part of Air

I wonder again what this is for — reproduction, gathering possessions, at last the disappearance into memories of friends aging so fast tears blow back from their eyes like big silly dogs holding their heads out of fast cars, noses to the wind.

I imagine clouded light, how wind shifts addresses into treetops, how birds make the meadow lively or quiet. I want to write each stalk and unfurled spade, leaves I knew when I was young, then lost for decades when I loved the world from inside rooms. I lean over the pond, its deep stillness unsettled by breeze. I age as light does. It falls as leaves.

Kansas Girl

Harp of her body thrums
with summer, cicada song
calls her home to supper.
Strong brown legs beat
across the wheatfield
carrying her in.

Someone switches on
a radio in the kitchen
and she knows
it will soon be time
for bed, her pink and white
curtains going gray
in ruffles of dusk.

July sings that it is almost
August in the voice of the train
traveling the city limits,
its three-note horn filtered
through trees full of dusty leaves
hanging like corpses of fruit.

Field

Washboard rows succumb to rhythm of too much
and not enough. Summer machines separate each
from each. Fall falls mostly shadows. And then in the cold
time, none. Sometimes the company of lightness
or frantic peck and crop. Increase voluptuous, tang
in the cells. Nurture. Dead things nuzzle in. Unconscious
geometry. Tongue rich, swish, whispers this root. Tumble.
Undoing.

How in winter the haunting is done

Time
Winter wheat in green rows, field keeps the score.
Not long before grass binds the plow.

Sky
River trees flap with leaves and blackbirds.
Cottonwoods age against the logic of seasons.

Bed
Narrow paths for deer's slender legs. Then, a tamped
swirl of flattened grass.

Gloaming
Collapsed house holds up one lampshade.
Sun catches its glass frill.

Wind
Brown shack cants north. Reasons hum in our ears.

Farm Wife

Old porch skirts this house,
its floor the exact center
of an orbit from which crows
arrow their black way
across a smear of sky.

Her old man stands against
the land, hands full of flight
he hoards in jars she pours out
every chance she gets.
Flies find their way in

through slashes in the screen.
Each slap of the door
sets off another round
of currents unsettling
around her faithless crop.

If they don't tell us

we will never know
the things farmers see
between the rows
where life's rough
beating beingness grows.

In the silence
of farmers we lose
what is real, leaving
the stories of soil
and sprout, ears
and snout to the
documentarians
crouched in rainforests,
city clothes clinging
to their backs.

In farmers' wordlessness
hides the truth
of food, exuberances
of planting and birth,
cleaving of harvest
and slaughter,
all the blood and bother
of bringing life
to our tables, this deep
green and butchered world
we browse and breathe.

Art History

Old man eats his Big Mac in the blue
McDonald's dining room. The frames
of his glasses are transparent. His feed cap
says Vermeer. What if other farmers somewhere
are wearing caps that say Rembrandt,
Caravaggio, Rubens? What if down at the co-op
they stand around the counter arguing color
and shadow instead of seed and till? The farmers
dream of dark lecture halls,
where they squint through dust floating
in a perfect cone of projector light,
straining to see just one curve
that tilts toward the baroque, a single
passage hinting at everything yet
to come, eyes hungry for the ripeness
they recognize as another kind of renaissance.

Dearest Little L,

I wish I could send you
this wonder of peonies.
Not a photograph or petal,
not a full bloom pressed
between pages of half the dictionary —
I mean the almost bitter
sweet scent, one bloom browning
next to a white flower's perfection
hiding a rumor of pink
at its center, loose sulfur
stamens against magenta
silk fragments fallen
to the table. When I look away
to write this, when I turn back,
I am lost to you sure as an ant
coursing such voluptuous chambers.

At the Museum of Flowers

When I say *zinnias* do you see them,
Mexico colors, in high Kansas summer
behind the red brick garage? Is your mother
freckling in the sun, holding a green
garden hose gushing water into the bed,
making creamy mud shine like icing?
Do monarchs light and flutter
from frilled bloom to bloom?
And can you lift them as your father
taught between your first grade fingers,
set one on each shoulder and
walk into the house wearing wings?
All that summer and deep
into September, will you visit zinnias
hunting for stolen flight?

World to Come

The mother is in full sun and finally
the poppies she could not grow in life
are blooming on thin stems, but
her lipstick is brighter. She is sitting
in a chair, hair still black, face freckling.

The father is steering across a swath
marked by saguaro. His eye in death
is God's — he sees at once the road,
land, sky, and himself unconscious
of driving. The only sound is breath.

Neither of them is smiling. They are
alone, as in life we never let them be.

In the Book of Old Pictures

For once they are not
smoking, the fact that will
kill them both, these fetching
not-yet-parents. Bare-
chested, he is my not-already
father, and she is caught
in the sparkle, pleased
with her trick of calling birds
from the tree. I believed
in charms before I learned
she could not do all
I wanted, my fingers
straining toward the robin
on the picket fence.
Those two people,
why did they make me?
I ask the photograph, black
and full. They are smiling.
They are paper, no more
than a trick of light on silver.

Not Yet Flying

The velvet bump
of tadpoles against my
palm, hundreds
of fat, black bodies
wiggling in the galvanized
tub, bodies my brother
planned to make bait or money.
My sister and I plotted
to release them,
half-legged and stubby tailed.
When we picked up the tub
between us, they sloshed
and plopped on the patio
like ripe cherries.

My brother sent
the bait man's three dollars
away with a comic book
coupon and we teased him
about the thick envelope
marked Joe Weider,
Trainer of Champions.
All that summer my brother
left his t-shirt on
to hide his belly.

My son's sharp shoulder
blades stick out like wings.
We go to find tadpoles.
I want to show him how
their comet shapes sprout
legs and front arms and
stand-up eyeballs.
We kneel beside the sandpit,
barely a ripple in the water,
only carp, and a throaty
vibration from a clutch
of frogs.

In the Book of Marvels

Magic of three beats a rhythm in my body,
a tilting symmetry in which the queen
visits three times her baby, the wolf
tries three ways to get inside, the
huntsman tracks the fawn for three
days. Here are the three in this story:

first, the cat purrs on my lap,
his sea-green eyes distant
as a planet where next clouds
break up and the blues
turn azure over the islands.
Then, a spotted fish leaps

from the garden pond. His golden tail
does not say that he has known all along
about the cat, the sky, and the stories
we tell; they're only a watery whisper of fins
and slippery skin, your own voice humming
in the dark, the marvelous colors of what is.

At the Museum of Possibility

The metal sculpture tiptoes around its glass box. A
stuffed owl flickers wing shadows across the ceiling
while a music box inside the lightning-struck tree keens
a melody. Every antique photograph drips midnight
perfume. *Where is the exit*, you ask the uniformed guard
who seems to be wearing the face of your first lover.
He invites you to ruffle his hair for old time's sake.
Mummies on the mantelpiece speak the hour. You find
the only postcards on offer are pictures of your own
sleeping form, knees and ribcage labeled in wavering
script: flight path and carousel.

Ologies

Every empty house unfolds a museum vibrating with invisible people who moved out. Cupboards hold their air of ago; corners exhale a haunted sigh. The bathtub faucet's silver handle pronounces dream words in its squeaky voice.

Bathroom
Pastel green tile, water stain in the tub, shard missing from the medicine chest mirror and inside, a slot for razor blades. Within the wall, deposited and forgotten: an archeology of jaws, messages from cheekbones and chins.

Dining room
Sunbeams cross floorboards, expose a crumb in a corner brushed from a sleeve. Dancing in the china cabinet, a tiny ballerina holds up a flower where the birthday candle goes.

Bedroom
Dents in sky blue carpet disclose where two beds stood. Cedar-lined closet preserves a spicy air of souvenir-shop rose pods. In a windowsill, a ladybug on its back fades toward yellow, black legs folded and folded.

There are no minor gods

Memory is a field of ruin,
a whatnot of darkling shards.
I am the wraith in rainy
trees. I am holding
my breath, riding the wild
bluegray back of the jay.
I am a ghost in the leaves.
I shall tell
what my childhood was —
counting ants all afternoon
and at night, the ticking
of one lost bat. Black
hornet falls through blossoms.

The Luminosity of Objects

Morning dapples old plates, painted furniture, a shelf full of silver. Like an eye, liquid reflections reveal a different house, the one people report after they go, whose leaning bookshelves and bottle-green velvet chair take on the gravity of myth. Cobwebs grow wise and the squat teapot sings its old story. An invisible clock winds down. Hear the ticking — each succeeding interval a sliver longer until you can't tell whether it's time or only you slipping like a nap into afternoon.

Some of the Rooms in the Hall of Desire

White
A child makes her way to the shrine in tree dark twilight. Stone children kneel before Our Lady of Fatima, but the girl crawls past them, uphill toward the glow of the lady. She is a wild thing in undergrowth where they say nuns bury miscarried babies. Night smells like wax and a tangle of hair.

Blues
Someone takes her hand and tries to lead her to the dance floor but her legs give in to tequila and she cannot dance past midnight, past rescue, past all the everything that came before.

Night
In the garden of the old lighthouse, she breaks off petals of ivory and orange, spilling them as if moonlight were cheap as a lady-slipper dropped from a tinker's pocket.

Bruise
Late night, almost dark, what's left of sunset is lavender gray and white buildings turn violet. The little girl whispers alone in her room. *Here kitty. Here kitty kitty.*

Requiem
She strays into the shallows with the heron. On the bed, her eiderdown breaks into leaf.

Letter to Virginia

Fill the jug with water and cut an armload of lilacs
deep with violet in every petal, each lobe entire
with purple. Go back into the garden wearing your
brimmed hat and when you spy the rabbit, so near
because you are so still, wheel your hat over it and
watch the black circle hop away. Consider the beam
of the lighthouse. Let it draw you onto the road home,
dropping stones from your pockets as you go.
Be your body, sufficient, again.

The Mortal Takes Herself Home

Despite the bloody gauze, the fire
injected along her veins, she exits
as she arrived, with the same complaint.
It took three hours to uncover it is not her
heart's determination to give
out. You are fine, the doctor assures
her and so she refuses his pills
for pain. She wants to ask for a heart
mender anyway, to slip into some sweet
hospital wing where the 60ish women
are soothed with fragrant teas and
the laying on of firm hands, unafraid
of breaking in. Reckless with mercy
for breaking out

Vo Ed

The boys from auto body school stand
circled, cigarettes in mouth or held loose
between thumb and finger in hands
scarred by sheet metal, pocked with body putty.

These are the boys they said couldn't hack it
in high school where turning pages and talk
equaled preparation for what teachers called
life. No Friday night football games and dances
in the gym with girls who might not later
admire the line of a fender, pull them
laughing and smooth into the back seat.

Not for these boys, their breathing expelled
into air, visible as exhaust. Here
are the men we'll take our cars to, the palms
of their hands tuned to undulations
of steel, and ask them to buff out all
our little lapses, and cheerfully
surrender our rough bodies to their skill.

At the Museum of Keys

Every room jingles like a school custodian and your task is to follow the sound until you find a door that fits the key you hold. O dreamer of locks, you've rubbed those fingers raw against the teeth of your responsibility, each a medal you haven't earned. When you arrive, having tried each latch, your room glitters and tinkles. You run your palm across each exhibit and set the metal singing. In the ringing, each key bears your fingerprint, lint from your particular pocket, residue from the compulsive bolts and jambs of your every day.

At the Museum of Trees

You pay your dime and get a ticket that promises a forest, a thicket, but when you push through the turnstile, you find a single pine. The one your parents were dropping into the hole, its balled roots tight, the morning your mother went into labor. The constant temperature is April and the needles are still new. A label reveals you will outlive the tree, gone shaggy with sudden height while you turn away to read the words. You know it's a curator's trick that seasons pass and reverse themselves as though you are too simple to understand. You stand here anyway, sapling to pinesap logs and sting of the chainsaw.

At the Museum of Lost Things

When she cracks open a window in this edifice without
doors, a jumble of the missing waits. Uncatalogued,
no labels reveal the dates. Each time she looks in, she sees
another thing, as if hands rearranged, acquired and culled
the collection, toiled in darkness. A doll lamp her mother
dressed in rosy fabric. Bright taste of clove. A specific green
dish photographed with snow and purple afternoon
blooming of the mirabilis flower. One slick gray booklet
called *Our Lady of Fatima* that came in the mail addressed
only to her.

If only once the summons were a roar

Bury this bronze, its angles forged
and beaten, but not until you clothe it
in chrysanthemum and rust. Unfold
your flesh and bite the brass cylinder,
delicate as a baby's finger. Wake, dreamer,
to the bones you hoard, to the medals
you desire, coin stamped deep
with animals' bodies. Was it claw
or feather the night you flung yourself
rough into desire's incisors? Swallow
down the bullet so you become a gun,
language in your throat, chambered.

Each November Day

Effervescent mist shivers across skin and here's what it is
to be champagne. Streets shine back the sun. Leaf shadow
catches on wings of birds lashing across air

gone amber. Sky is whispering that every wind-bound
leaf, every autumn minute unfurls. Today it's coins
in the air, no matter where you look, drifting piles of sighs

underfoot, spangling grass with currency of spent
chlorophyll. A cat the color of weather, his tawny fur
in summer transformed by earth's tipping

axis to a pelt the pashas would envy, comes trotting over
lawns to fill his hungry belly at any back door.
Behind each fugitive gleam tilting toward cold crouches

the draught of days we have sipped before but never with
this hum in our marrow that says despite everything,
we are here only to squander all this gold.

Notes

The title "as confirmation – echo –" is from Carl Phillips's essay "Boon and Burden: Identity in Contemporary American Poetry." Thanks to Joel for conversations that prompted this poem.

In "She Named His Coming," the line "whoever goes to shroud her do no harm" is a slight revision of the first line of John Donne's "The Funeral."

"Not Yet Flying" takes its title from Paul Klee's 1927 drawing, *Hardly Still Walking, Not Yet Flying.*

"There are no minor gods" takes its title from Gaston Bachelard's sentence, "For the decidedly mythic life, there are no minor gods."

"If only once the summons were a roar" is a line from Jim Harrison's poem "Complaint."

Lori Brack's Kansas roots coil down to her mother's Barton County homestead and her father's Russian-German immigrant parents. Her work background includes newspaper journalism, contemporary art education, public library programming, and college teaching. In 2010, the Field School, New York, published her chapbook *A Fine Place to See the Sky,* a poetic script for a work of performance art by Ernesto Pujol. The script is a collaboration with her grandfather's 1907-1918 Kansas farming journals.

This project was made possible, in part, by generous support from the Osage Arts Community.

Osage Arts Community provides temporary time, space and support for the creation of new artistic works in a retreat format, serving creative people of all kinds — visual artists, composers, poets, fiction and nonfiction writers. Located on a 152-acre farm in an isolated rural mountainside setting in Central Missouri and bordered by ¾ of a mile of the Gasconade River, OAC provides residencies to those working alone, as well as welcoming collaborative teams, offering living space and workspace in a country environment to emerging and mid-career artists. For more information, visit us at www.oac.com

Osage Arts Community

www.ingramcontent.com/pod-product-compliance
Lightning Source LLC
Chambersburg PA
CBHW021451080526
44588CB00009B/796